American Sign Language

American Sign Language

Deborah Kent

Franklin Watts
A Division of Scholastic Inc.
New York • Toronto • London • Auckland • Sydney
Mexico City • New Delhi • Hong Kong
Danbury, Connecticut

Note to readers: Definitions for words in **bold** can be found in the Glossary at the back of this book.

Photographs © 2003: Anne Clarke Berube: 48; Corbis Images: 29 (Hulton-Deutsch Collection), 2 (Richard T. Nowitz), 36 (Glenn Waggner), 23; Ellen B. Senisi: cover, 26; Gallaudet University Archives: 14, 18, 20, 21, 30; Getty Images/Roger Viollet: 16; Hulton|Archive/Getty Images: 12; Martha's Vineyard Historical Society: 8; North Wind Picture Archives: 35; Photo Researchers, NY/Will and Deni McIntyre: 34; PhotoEdit: 47 (Jeff Greenberg), 39, 53 (Will Hart), 10, 51 (Robin Sachs); Stock Boston/David J. Sams: 42; Stock Montage, Inc.: 44; Stone/Getty Images/Robert E. Daemmrich: 40; Superstock, Inc.: 6; The Image Works: 50 (Peter Hvizdak), 11 (Jack Kurtz), 41 (Ellen Senisi); Tom Pantages: 32.

The photograph on the cover shows a boy signing to a friend. The photograph opposite the title page shows a teacher teaching sign language to a group of students.

Library of Congress Cataloging-in-Publication Data

Kent, Deborah.
    American sign language / by Deborah Kent.
        p. cm. — (Watts library)
    Summary: Explores the history of American Sign Language and deaf culture, including ongoing controversies within the deaf community today.
    ISBN 0-531-12018-X (lib. bdg.)   0-531-16662-7 (pbk.)
    1. American Sign Language—Juvenile literature. 2. Deaf—Means of communication—United States—Juvenile literature. [1. American Sign Language. 2. Deaf. 3. People with disabilities.] I. Title. II. Series.
HV2476 .K46 2003
419'.7—dc21

2002008882

Contents

A strong deaf community developed on the island of Martha's Vineyard in the 1800s.

Chapter One

Language for the Eyes

The island of Martha's Vineyard lies in the Atlantic Ocean off Cape Cod. During the 1800s the islanders lived in isolation, having little contact with people from the mainland. Hereditary deafness was widespread in the communities on Martha's Vineyard. In 1880, one out of four people in the village of Chilmark was deaf.

On clear mornings the Chilmark fishing fleet scattered across the bay. With teamwork born of long experience, each

This photograph shows the Chilmark Schoolhouse on Martha's Vineyard.

crew set out its nets. When one boat approached another, crew members paused in their work to ask questions and exchange news. Their voices could not carry across the wind and waves, but that didn't matter. With their hands, faces, and bodies, they conveyed their thoughts in a series of movements.

"How's your catch today?" one man might ask. And the answer would flash back over the water, "Not so good. We're heading farther out."

Three out of four people in Chilmark could hear. But nearly everyone had a deaf parent or a deaf sister, a deaf uncle or a deaf child. Most hearing people were fully bilingual. They used spoken English, but they also learned sign language as a matter of course. Conversation in Chilmark slid from sign to English and back to sign again. No one seemed to notice or care.

American Sign Language (ASL) is a system of hand shapes and movements combined with facial expressions and body postures. Like any other language, ASL has a vocabulary and its own sentence structure and complex rules of grammar. Fluent signers can express the full range of human thought and emotion with their hands and bodies.

In general, people who are profoundly deaf from early childhood face great barriers to learning to speak and lip-read. Without the aid of hearing, they must learn oral language through one labored step after another. In contrast, deaf children master ASL swiftly and naturally by watching other signers, much as hearing children master spoken language by listening and imitation.

Because they share a language and life experience in common, deaf people who sign feel a deep sense of community. ASL carries the traditions, the humor, and the poetry of Deaf culture from one generation to the next.

"Deaf" with a Capital D

When a person loses his hearing later in life, he usually keeps the ability to speak aloud, even though he can no longer hear his own words. Most likely he will continue to use spoken and written language as his chief means of communication. Within the ASL community such people are sometimes referred to as "deaf" with a small d. The term "Deaf" with a capital D is reserved for those who consider ASL to be their primary language. Members of the Deaf community do not regard their deafness as a disability. They consider themselves part of a cultural group, much like Latinos, Korean-Americans, or people of Italian heritage.

A speech therapist works with deaf students.

Today teachers, legislators, and the general public recognize ASL as a legitimate language. Some feel it is the birthright of every deaf child in the United States. But American Sign Language has not always been so well regarded. For decades it was scorned by educators of the deaf, who forbade its use by their students. The history of ASL is a story of prejudice, fear, and good intentions gone wrong. And it is the story of a minority group that banded together for mutual support, its members sustained by a language they continue to share and cherish.

Despite its difficult history, ASL flourishes today.

Charles Michel, Abbe de L'Épée, was an early advocate for educating the deaf.

Chapter Two

Seeing Words

Until the middle of the 1700s, few deaf people ever received a formal education. Those who lived in the country were usually isolated among relatives and neighbors who could hear and who relied upon speech to communicate. These deaf people learned to communicate their basic needs through **pantomime**, but they could not truly converse and exchange ideas.

For deaf people who lived in cities, however, life took on richness and depth. In European cities such as Paris and London, deaf people found one another and formed close-knit communities.

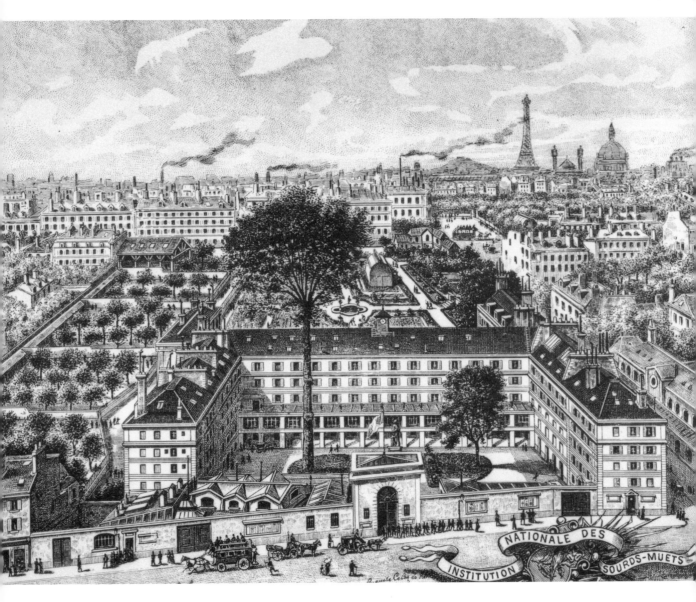

This illustration shows L'Épée's school for the deaf.

Each city developed its own form of sign language, which deaf people passed down from one generation to the next.

In 1755 a French priest, Charles Michel, Abbe de L'Épée, founded the National Institution for the Deaf in Paris, the first school for deaf children in France. Abbe de L'Épée saw the

Teaching the Teacher

Two of the early pupils at the school in Paris, sisters deaf from birth, taught their form of sign language to de L'Épée.

deaf as lost souls to be brought to God. He wanted to teach them the principles of Christianity.

De L'Épée quickly realized that his students arrived with the ability to communicate. "Every deaf-mute sent to us already has a language," he wrote. "With it he expresses his needs, desires, pains, and so on, and makes no mistake when others express themselves likewise."

De L'Épée had mixed feelings about sign language. He recognized its enormous value to the deaf community. Yet he worried because it was radically different from spoken French. Using the language of his students as a basis, he added French grammar and created **Signed French**. De L'Épée used Signed French in his classrooms. But on their own, the students returned to their old communication system, which came to be known as **French Sign Language** (FSL). FSL grammar was very different from that of spoken French, as it used the natural flow and rhythms of gesture.

The school for the deaf in Paris served as a model for many other institutions throughout western Europe. These schools used sign languages that varied from country to country and even from one city to another. Yet many teachers of the deaf looked down on sign languages as inferior to speech. They had trouble believing that a purely visual

language could be as valid as their own spoken one. Jean-Marc Itard, who taught at the Paris school in the 1790s, called FSL "that barbaric language without pronouns, without conjunctions, without any of the words that permit us to express abstract ideas."

Who Learns to Speak?

Hearing children (children who can hear) learn to speak by listening to, and imitating, the people around them. Because deaf children do not hear speech, they cannot learn to speak in this natural way. With extensive training and effort, some deaf children learn to lip-read and to speak clearly enough to be understood. Successful oral students are usually those who have the necessary hearing or who became deaf after they began learning to talk. Children who are profoundly deaf from birth or infancy seldom become comfortable with speech as a primary means of communication. Yet when they are exposed to a language based on signs, they learn it as swiftly as hearing children learn speech.

Educators Against Sign Language

One group of educators, known as oralists, believed that deaf children should not be allowed to use any form of sign language. These teachers thought deaf pupils should learn to speak and to lip-read. They argued that deaf people who signed could only communicate with others who knew sign language. In contrast, deaf students who mastered spoken language could function in hearing society.

Teachers in Great Britain strongly favored the oral approach. Britain's leading school for the deaf was Braidwood Academy. The Braidwood family claimed great success in teaching speech and lip-reading. Few Braidwood pupils, however, had been deaf from birth. It is unknown whether their training was effective with children who were profoundly deaf from infancy.

The newly formed United States had no schools for the deaf. Because the nation was largely rural, most deaf children grew up in isolation, with little chance to learn about the world.

After his success with Alice, Thomas Hopkins Gallaudet went on to study different teaching methods abroad.

Signs for a New Nation

On a mild summer day in 1812, a theology student named Thomas Hopkins Gallaudet visited his neighbor Dr. Mason Cogswell. The Cogswells and the Gallaudets were among the most prominent families in Hartford, Connecticut. After dinner Gallaudet sat outdoors with Cogswell's nine-year-old daughter, Alice. Alice was a bright, inquisitive little girl who lost her hearing from an illness at the age of two.

As Alice watched, Gallaudet took off his hat and held it out. Then he wrote the word HAT in the dirt with a stick. He pointed at the word, then at the hat, trying to show Alice that the marks on the ground stood for the object in his hand. At last, with a burst of excitement, Alice caught on. She grabbed the stick and wrote HAT in the dirt. Then she dropped the hat over the word she had written.

In that moment Gallaudet knew that Alice understood the concept of language.

Mason Cogswell was thrilled by his daughter's progress. Eventually he sent Gallaudet to England to study with the Braidwoods. He hoped Gallaudet would start a school for deaf children in Hartford on his return. But Gallaudet was disappointed by his reception at Braidwood Academy. The Braidwoods jealously guarded their special training methods, and refused to share them with this American upstart.

After months of frustration Gallaudet went to France to learn what he could about French teaching methods. Unlike the Braidwoods, the French teachers gave him a warm welcome. Gallaudet was impressed by the work of the Royal Institute for Deaf-Mutes, and quickly learned the basics of Signed French. When he was ready to go back to Hartford, he invited one of the French teachers to come with him to help

American Born

An American forerunner of ASL is sometimes called Old American Sign Language. Some of its signs may have come from a gestural system used as a common language in trade and council by Native American tribes in the New England region.

Laurent Clerc returned to the United States with Gallaudet to help found a new school for the deaf.

him found a new school. The teacher was a brilliant deaf man named Laurent Clerc. On the journey across the Atlantic Ocean, Clerc began teaching FSL to Gallaudet.

Back in Hartford, Clerc and Gallaudet set to work. They

raised funds, trained teachers, and recruited deaf students. In 1817 the Connecticut Asylum for the Education and Instruction of Deaf and Dumb Persons opened with twenty-one pupils.

At the Connecticut Asylum, Clerc and Gallaudet taught the students using French Sign Language. But some of the American children already had a sign language of their own. They added many new words and rules of grammar to FSL. The Hartford students shaped and molded the language of the Paris streets. As time passed, FSL evolved to become American Sign Language, or ASL.

This photograph shows the Connecticut Asylum for the Education and Instruction of Deaf and Dumb Persons. The school, which still exists today, is now called the American School for the Deaf.

21

More Schools for the Deaf

In the decades before the Civil War, schools for the deaf opened in nearly every state. Most took the Hartford school as their model. Classes were taught in American Sign Language and in **Signed English**, a **manual language** based on standard English word order. The majority of the teachers in these schools were deaf themselves. Inside and outside class, they conducted spirited discussions on philosophy, history, literature, and art. The students flourished. With ASL as their native language, they mastered written English as a second language. The students had full access to the written thought of the Western world.

As more and more students completed their studies at state-run **residential schools**, or boarding schools, for the deaf, the brightest longed to continue their studies. In 1864 Edward Miner Gallaudet, Thomas Gallaudet's son, helped to found Gallaudet College, a unique institution on a wooded tract of land in Washington, D.C. It was the first school of higher education adapted to the special needs of deaf students.

High Honors

The charter for Gallaudet College was signed by President Abraham Lincoln at the height of the Civil War. Only the most qualified applicants were admitted. Applicants had to pass a daunting series of entrance exams on a number of subjects, including Latin, physiology, and philosophy. Few high school seniors today, hearing or deaf, could show such mastery of these subjects.

Edward Miner Gallaudet followed in his father's footsteps by helping to found a school for the deaf. Now known as Gallaudet University, the school attracts students from around the world.

Conflict Over ASL

Not all teachers and parents were happy with the use of ASL in the schools. Some educators **staunchly** believed that deaf students should speak, not sign. The controversy between oral and sign communication reached the boiling point in 1880. At a meeting in Milan, Italy, known as the International Congress on the Education of the Deaf, a group of teachers of the deaf voted to ban the use of sign languages among deaf students. Deaf teachers were forbidden to attend the meeting. Only teachers who could hear, teachers who would probably favor oral teaching methods, were allowed to cast their votes. As one British teacher wrote later, "The victory for the cause of pure speech was gained before the Congress began."

The president of the congress, an Italian priest named Giulio Tarra, delivered an impassioned address. His fiery words condemned sign languages as the crude gestures of the godless and ignorant, and depicted speech as having God's blessing. "Oral speech is the sole power that can rekindle the light that God breathed into man," Tarra declared. He insisted that no signs could represent such ideas as faith, hope, justice, virtue, or the soul. "Speech alone," Tarra proclaimed, "divine itself, is the right way to speak of divine matters."

The Milan congress received overwhelming support from hearing teachers everywhere. Deaf teachers were forced out of the classroom. Speech training filled class schedules, edging out such subjects as arithmetic, geography, and even reading.

Statistics tell a grim story. In 1867, thirteen years before the Milan conference, the United States had twenty-six schools for the deaf. Most of the teachers were deaf, and ASL was the language of instruction. Four decades later all that had changed. In 1907 the United States boasted 139 schools for the deaf. Nearly all of the teachers could hear, and all of the schools forbade their students to sign.

In classrooms throughout the country, teachers smacked signing hands with rulers. If a child persisted in signing, the teacher tied her hands behind her back. All eyes had to look toward the front of the room and follow the movements of the teacher's lips. Every pupil had to struggle to form the sounds of spoken words.

Educators did everything in their power to destroy ASL. Yet they were never able to overcome the resistance of deaf people, who simply used the language in secret. ASL continued as deaf people passed down the language from one generation to the next.

In the early 1900s, students were not allowed to use sign language in school. Today, students using sign language can be found everywhere from the classroom to the playground.

Chapter Three

A Living Language

In 1927 a twelve-year-old boy named David Wright enrolled at a school for the deaf in England. All of the teachers spoke English and urged the pupils to communicate through speech. But the moment the teacher's back was turned, the students burst into sign. "Confusion stuns the eye," Wright wrote years later in his memoir. "Arms whirl like windmills in a hurricane. The emphatic, silent vocabulary of the body—look, expression, bearing, glance of eye—form their pantomime, absolutely engrossing pandemonium. . . . What I have been describing is how we talked when no hearing person was present. At such times . . . we relaxed inhibitions, wore no masks."

Out of the Closet

For more than sixty years ASL persisted underground, despite the tireless efforts of teachers to stamp it out. Students signed to one another in the hallways, bathrooms, and dormitories of schools for the deaf. The foremost teachers of ASL were the deaf children of deaf parents, who learned to sign at home from infancy onward. When they went away to school, these expert signers quickly taught ASL to their classmates. Since there were few deaf teachers at the schools for the deaf, and since not many hearing parents learned ASL, deaf children seldom had the chance to learn signing from adults. Linguists noted that sign languages are the only languages on Earth primarily taught to children by other children.

Throughout the United States a tragic paradox existed at schools for the deaf. The students could not understand or express themselves in spoken English, the language of their teachers. The teachers could not use or understand ASL, the language of their students. Even the most basic exchange of information was a struggle. Ted Supalla, a research psychologist, describes his experience at the school for the deaf in the state of Washington:

"We had speech training every day. Sat in front of a mirror

A young girl works on her speech with an instructor.

and worked and worked. We watched ourselves in the mirror. 'Flag is red. Flag is blue.' Over and over. We wore headphones. Watched the blackboard. The following year we did it all again. The janitor was deaf. [We] used to find him and talk to him."

After graduation most students tended to stay in towns near the school for the deaf or to move to cities that had large deaf populations. Within these deaf communities people

While much of the educational community supported speech and lip-reading, Edward Miner Gallaudet advocated the use of American Sign Language in teaching the deaf.

worked, married, and raised their children. Common experience and a common language, ASL, bound deaf people together.

After the Congress of Milan, when ASL was being extinguished in American classrooms, one leading educator of the deaf held firm. Edward Miner Gallaudet fought to preserve ASL at Gallaudet College. Because his mother was deaf and his father was fluent in ASL, Edward Gallaudet was a native signer. At the Milan congress he suggested that sign languages should be used for the teaching of all academic subjects, while speech and lip-reading should be taught after regular school hours. Though the congress voted down his proposal, he carried it forward at Gallaudet. While Edward Gallaudet served as president, all course work at the college was conducted in ASL. Students could study spoken English as a second language.

Over time, however, ASL lost its foothold even at Gallaudet. In the college classrooms, ASL was replaced by Signed English, a manual language that is somewhat similar to de L'Épée's Signed French. Signed English follows the word order of spoken English and requires the same use of English articles, conjunctions, and prepositions. Gallaudet teachers regarded Signed English as the "best" form of sign language, since it was modeled upon the spoken language of mainstream culture.

Though they used Signed English in class, most students at Gallaudet turned to ASL when they conversed among themselves. ASL gave them an ease and freedom they never found with Signed English. In ASL they joked, courted, mourned, and told stories.

In 1955 a soft-spoken professor of English named William Stokoe joined the faculty at Gallaudet. While living in Scotland, Stokoe had become interested in the various dialects spoken by its rural people. His interest expanded to a passion for all minority languages, languages that persist in small populations within the larger society. When he arrived at Gallaudet, Stokoe marveled at the movements and gestures of his deaf students. He could scarcely believe what he saw. Here was a minority language no scholar had yet discovered. With the help of several students, Stokoe flung himself into the study of ASL.

To Stokoe's amazement, most of the other teachers thought he was wasting his time. The students themselves shook their heads in disbelief at his interest in their language. They insisted that ASL was nothing but a series of crude gestures used by children. It was not really a language at all. When Stokoe published his first article on ASL, "Sign Language Structure," in 1960, the Gallaudet community grew

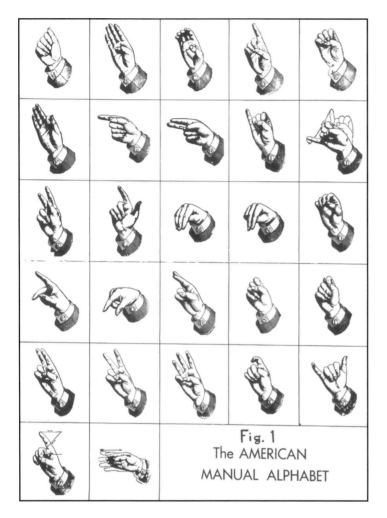

Fig. 1
The AMERICAN
MANUAL ALPHABET

A page from Stokoe's dictionary shows the signs for the different letters of the alphabet.

indignant. "They thought I was crazy," Stokoe told a reporter years later. "Not just a little odd; clinically insane. I suppose it was a good thing I had tenure."

Stokoe did not give up, and gradually his ideas took hold. In 1965 he and a group of Gallaudet students published an ASL dictionary, the first to appear since 1918. Their work proved that ASL was a true language with a complex grammar all its own. It had distinct parts of speech, such as nouns, verbs, adjectives, and adverbs. It had unique idioms, set phrases that convey an idea, question, or command beyond the meaning of the individual words. Signers even made puns, playfully mixing similar signs that had different meanings.

Stokoe's work sparked excitement among linguists around

Train Gone

In a lively ASL discussion, an inexperienced signer cannot keep up. If he asks the others to slow down they may sign, "Train gone. Sorry." This idiom means it is too late, and there is no time to go back.

the world. Until that time, most scholars assumed that all true languages were based on speech. Stokoe proved that speech was not necessary at all; language could be purely visual. The eye, like the ear, could receive and interpret symbols. The hands could speak as eloquently as the tongue.

In the Deaf community annoyance over Stokoe's work turned to astonishment, and finally jubilation. After nearly a century of suppression, ASL regained its rightful place as the language of deaf people in the United States. Public recognition of ASL brought deaf people a sense of pride and solidarity they had never known before.

Learning the Basics

In 1827 Laurent Clerc wrote that the only way to learn ASL is to practice with a fluent signer. Books teach the signs for specific words and explain points of grammar. But like any other language, ASL is more than a set of words and rules. Among native signers it takes on a life of its own.

ASL is made up of thousands of signs that symbolize many different things, such as actions, objects, and characteristics. Each sign is composed of one or more "hand shapes," often combined with hand movement, facial expression, and body gestures. Some signs are formed with one hand, and some with two. The position of the hands in relation to the body is crucial. Most signs are formed in front of the chest, but some involve touching the face, shoulders, ears, or other body parts.

A signer does not rely on her hands alone. She uses her

A woman makes the sign for "touch."

How Do You Sign It?

Sky: Spreading the hand palm outward at forehead level, make a sweeping motion from left to right.

Cat: Touch the right cheek with thumb and forefinger and draw the hand outward to represent whiskers.

entire body to convey her meaning. When she describes a sad event, her shoulders sag, her mouth droops, and her signs grow heavy and slow. When she speaks of anger, she thrusts her shoulders forward and signs in quick, jabbing thrusts. The way a person signs reflects his personality, just as a hearing person's personality is often revealed in speech patterns. A tense, rigid person may sign with tight movements close to the body. A person who is easygoing and relaxed may sign with large, loose gestures that seem to reach out to the world.

Finger spelling is an essential component of ASL. Each letter of the alphabet is represented by a hand shape that somewhat resembles the letter's printed form. Finger spelling is used for the names of people and places and for words that do not have specific signs.

After receiving her award, Marlee Matlin makes a sign that means "I love you."

Chapter Four

Language Under Siege

On an evening in 1987 an actress named Marlee Matlin stepped to the podium to receive an Academy Award for her role in the movie *Children of a Lesser God*. Matlin, who is deaf, began her acceptance speech in ASL. Then she lowered her hands to her sides and broke into spoken English. Most of the people in the audience were deeply moved by Matlin's labored words. Yet her speech outraged many members of the Deaf community. In front of millions of viewers, Matlin had chosen speech over sign. By turning to speech, she had yielded to the demands of the hearing world. These responses to Marlee Matlin's Oscar acceptance highlight the age-old debate between sign and speech in the education of deaf people. Though ASL is more widely respected than ever before, the controversy still lingers for deaf people and their families.

Speech or Sign?

When parents learn that their baby is deaf, they ask themselves a host of questions. How will they communicate with a child who cannot hear them call his name? How will they explain the world to a child who cannot speak their language? Searching for answers, they take their child to a series of specialists. Some of these professionals, who are themselves hearing people, recommend training in speech and lip-reading. Others recommend ASL. As parents learn about ASL, they are impressed by its grace and beauty, but they do not understand this visual language and doubt that they can learn. ASL is so different from spoken English that it makes many hearing parents uncomfortable. Furthermore, teachers falsely warn that if a child begins to use signs, he will never learn to talk.

Children who have some usable hearing usually benefit from hearing aids and speech training. Children who are post-lingually deaf—who lose their hearing after they have learned some words—are also candidates for learning oral language. But for the thousands of people who are pre-lingually deaf—

profoundly deaf from a time before learning language—
speech training is an exercise in frustration.

    Pre-lingually deaf children who are taught by oral methods
tend to fall far behind their hearing peers in school. One study
found that the average deaf high school student read on the
third-grade level.

A teacher uses sign and speech with a deaf student during a speech class.

A parent and child communicate using ASL.

A parent and child communicate using ASL.

Interestingly, the most successful deaf students are those who have deaf parents. Because they learn ASL naturally at home, they enter school with a firm basis in language. With this foundation they more easily master written English.

Total Communication

The teacher stands before the class, speaking clearly and distinctly. As she speaks, she also signs. Her deaf pupils watch her hands and face, drawing her meaning from her signs and from her moving lips.

During the 1970s the education of deaf children embraced a new approach called **total communication**. In a total communication classroom the students are taught in speech and sign at the same time. The sign language used is generally Signed English, which allows the teacher to use spoken

In a total communication classroom, a teacher speaks the word "red" while making the sign for the word.

English word order. The use of Signed English enables the students to learn visually and to gain a knowledge of English grammar and structure. Some total communication teachers use Pidgeon Signed English (PSE), which also follows English word order, but leaves out articles, such as "the," and word endings that indicate verb tense and plurals.

Cued speech, another communication system, combines speech and hand shapes, positions, and movements. In this system, the speaker uses hand shapes, positions, and movements along with lip movements that convey speech sounds. Without the physical aspect of this system, the deaf person might have a difficult time understanding what was being said. Many sounds in English, such as "p," "b," and "m," look the same on the speaker's lips. Hand shapes, movements, and positions indicate what speech sound is being made. A hearing person can learn to use cued speech within a relatively short time.

Most people who regard ASL as their primary language enlist the help of sign-language interpreters when they deal with the hearing culture. Hospitals, police departments, schools, and other institutions often have interpreters on staff. In some instances, the deaf person hires an interpreter to go with him to appointments or to help him on the job. Many ASL interpreters are the hearing children of deaf parents. Completely bilingual in both spoken English and ASL, they are ideally suited to work as interpreters.

Speak Directly

When communicating with a deaf person through an interpreter, look at the deaf person and speak to her directly. The interpreter's job is to relay whatever you and the deaf person say to one another without changing anything that is said.

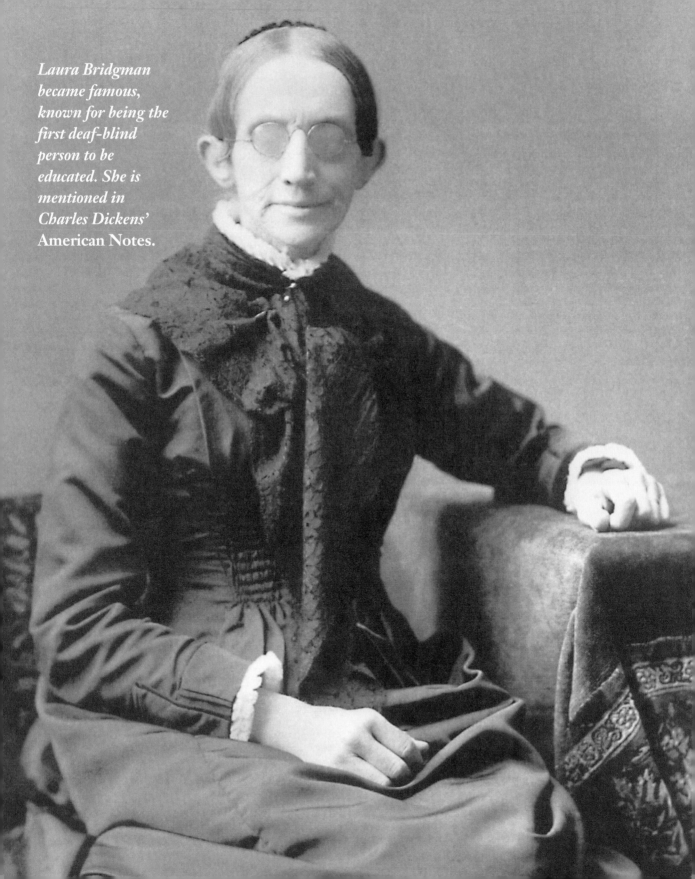

Laura Bridgman became famous, known for being the first deaf-blind person to be educated. She is mentioned in Charles Dickens' American Notes.

Chapter Five

Keys to Communication

In 1837 Dr. Samuel Gridley Howe launched the education of a seven-year-old girl named Laura Bridgman. At the age of two Laura lost both her sight and her hearing after a severe case of scarlet fever. Howe's work with Laura convinced him that human beings have an innate ability to develop language. Though she could neither see nor hear, Laura had created many signs that helped her communicate with her family. She touched her chin to indicate "Father," referring to her

Pioneering at Perkins

Laura Bridgman was the first deaf-blind child ever to be educated. At the Perkins Institution for the

Blind in Boston she learned to finger-spell, read, and write in English.

father's bristly beard. Two index fingers pressed together meant "same."

Since Howe's work with Laura, scientists have confirmed that all children have the need, and the ability, to use language. For many children the first and most natural language is a system of signs.

Bridging the Gap

Not all hearing children can readily master spoken language. Children with autism or severe mental retardation are often delayed in learning to speak, though they struggle to communicate their wants and ideas. Without speech, such children fall farther and farther behind their peers, and become increasingly frustrated and withdrawn.

During the 1970s some educators and parents experimented by teaching signs to hearing children with language difficulties. Most of these children picked up signs easily and began to use them in a natural, spontaneous way. Signing opened the door to communication for the first time.

For centuries educators had debated the use of signs with children who were deaf. Now the use of signs with hearing children added fuel to the age-old controversy. Opponents

argued that if autistic and retarded children were encouraged to sign, they wouldn't bother learning to talk.

Those who favored teaching signs argued that what these children needed most was language, language in any form. Once they could communicate, they would relate to others and learn about the world. Signing could even pave the way for learning spoken language later on.

College professor Michael Berube weighed these pros and

A caretaker teaches sign language to a boy with cerebral palsy who cannot talk.

Michael Berube and his son Jamie enjoy a book together. Sign language allows Jamie to communicate more freely with his parents.

cons when he considered teaching signs to his son Jamie. Jamie, who was born with Down syndrome, had trouble co-ordinating his lip and tongue movements. Speech was hard for Jamie to master, but his parents felt he had a lot to say. When they encouraged him to sign, they discovered they were right. "Those hearing children who learn to sign as a kind of tide-me-over measure turn out only to be hungrier for speech when their bodies finally allow them to produce it," Berube writes. "They know what it is to communicate verbally, they know their parents, siblings, and friends do it, and they know that by signing they've become a player in the language game as well. When they learn to speak, they have two languages at their command."

Stage and Story

Paul Preston is a fluent signer, the son of deaf parents. When he was invited to address a large group of deaf people at a conference, he realized he had to give his presentation in the Deaf way. "This meant identifying myself through my parents," he wrote later, "using American Sign Language without voice, addressing the audience interactively and informally, asking questions, and drawing from a rich history of [ASL] traditions." ASL users have their own unique way of delivering speeches, performing plays, and even singing.

As Paul Preston explains, ASL storytelling is a total experience. "Deaf storytelling does not 'boil down to a punch line,'" he explains. "The story is in the telling." When telling a story to friends, a signer brings the events to life with her hands, face, and body. She becomes each of the characters involved, recreating their gestures, attitudes, and feelings. Professional ASL storytellers perform at theaters, churches, and schools.

When the National Theatre of the Deaf (NTD) was founded in Connecticut in 1967, the group performed before deaf audiences using Signed English. From time to time, however, some of the actors would lapse into ASL. Audiences loved it and begged for more. In 1973 NTD gave its first full-scale

Show Time

In addition to NTD, several other companies perform regularly in ASL. Among them are the Cleveland Signstage Theatre, Deaf West Theatre, and the Sunshine Too National Touring Company.

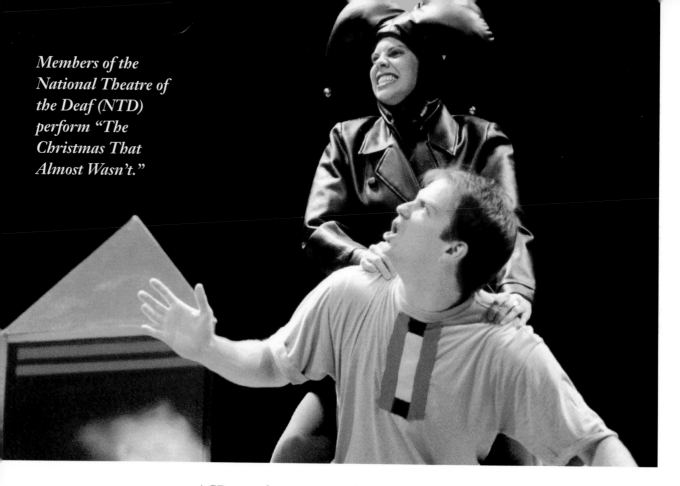

Members of the National Theatre of the Deaf (NTD) perform "The Christmas That Almost Wasn't."

Silent Song

Some churches and organizations of the deaf sponsor ASL choirs. Members sign the song lyrics together, creating rhythms and harmony in movement.

ASL production. Today NTD tours worldwide and performs for both deaf and hearing crowds using ASL and spoken words.

Several plays and films have included signing deaf actors who play deaf characters. The Tony Award-winning play *Children of a Lesser God* starred Phyllis Frelich, a native user of ASL. Director Peter Sellars has cast deaf actors in productions for hearing audiences and also collaborated with deaf playwright Shanny Mow on a production staged by NTD. "There is an extra dimension in the work of deaf actors," comments Sellars. "[They] are aware of the miracle of getting an idea across."

What Will the Future Bring?

In 1973 a new law called the Education for All Handicapped Children Act declared that children with disabilities should be taught in "the least restrictive setting possible." To most parents and educators, the least restrictive setting was the child's local public school. The new law held out the promise that disabled children could at last join the **mainstream**, that they would be fully integrated into the larger community.

Many deaf adults were dismayed by the new legislation. They worried that deaf children would not learn to sign if they went to public schools with hearing children. Cut off from

A teacher talks with a deaf girl in a mainstream classroom.

others who used ASL, they would grow up in isolation, not learning any language at all.

For generations, residential schools for the deaf kept ASL alive. Now **mainstreaming** threatened to deplete the residential programs and unravel the signing community. As mainstreaming became widespread, deaf adults went into action. Today they reach out to the hearing parents of deaf children, encouraging them to learn and use ASL. They organize picnics, parties, and other events where deaf children and deaf adults can meet. The deaf community works tirelessly to insure that ASL will survive and flourish in coming generations.

Another development that may have an impact on ASL is a medical procedure called the **cochlear implant**. The cochlea is part of the inner ear. In the 1990s researchers created an artificial cochlea that could be surgically implanted in deaf children. Doctors hoped that the surgery would provide a useful level of hearing to children who were deaf from birth. However, critics argue that for children with implants sound is highly distorted. Children who have had the operation are neither hearing nor deaf, and fall into a void somewhere between the two communities. Because they are not considered deaf, they may never learn ASL.

All over the world cultural minorities fight to preserve their native languages. The Basques in Spain, the French in Canada, the Kurds in Turkey, all believe passionately that their language and their identity are bound together. Just as other

ASL 101

In the mid-1980s high schools in Minneapolis allowed students to fulfill their modern language requirement by studying ASL. Today ASL classes are offered to hearing students in many high schools and colleges.

Two students converse
in ASL in the hallway
of their school.

minorities struggle to preserve their language, the Deaf community strives to protect and promote the use of ASL. ASL is far more than a method of communication. It is an eloquent form of expression, carrying the unique history of a people long misunderstood by the larger society. American Sign Language is part of our nation's irreplaceable heritage and a testament to human diversity.

Timeline

1755	Charles Michel, Abbe de L'Épée, founds the National Institution for the Deaf in Paris.
1812	Thomas Hopkins Gallaudet begins teaching Alice Cogswell, a deaf child, in Hartford, Connecticut.
1817	Thomas Hopkins Gallaudet and Laurent Clerc found a school for deaf children in Hartford. American Sign Language (ASL) develops at the Hartford school.
1837	Dr. Samuel Gridley Howe begins the education of Laura Bridgman, the first deaf-blind student to learn language.
1864	Abraham Lincoln signs the charter establishing Gallaudet College, the world's first college for deaf students, in Washington, D.C.
1880	Hearing educators gather at the International Congress on the Education of the Deaf and decide to ban sign languages from schools for the deaf throughout the world.
Early 1900s	Schools for the deaf forbid students to sign. Students teach one another ASL in secret.
1960	William Stokoe publishes "Sign Language Structure," demonstrating that ASL is a true language.
1973	Congress passes the Education for All Handicapped Children Act, declaring that children with disabilities must be educated in the least restrictive setting possible.
1970s	Teachers of the deaf employ total communication or the "whole language approach," combining speech with signs.
1990s	Cochlear implants become available, surgically improving the hearing of some deaf children and adults.

Glossary

American Sign Language—a manual language that developed among deaf people in the United States, based in part upon French Sign Language

cochlear implant—a surgically implanted device that helps restore hearing to some deaf people

cued speech—a communication system that combines lip-reading and hand shapes, positions, and movements

finger spelling—a manual alphabet

French Sign Language—a manual language that developed among deaf people in France and later formed the basis of American Sign Language

mainstreaming—the practice of educating children with disabilities in regular classes along with nondisabled peers

manual language—any language based on signs made with the hands

pantomime—communication through gestures, body movements, and facial expressions

residential school—a boarding school, such as the state-run schools for deaf children established in the nineteenth century

Signed English—a manual language based on English grammatical structure

Signed French—a manual language based on French grammatical structure

staunchly—firmly

total communication—a system of educating deaf children through the use of both speech and signs

To Find Out More

Books

Davis, Lennard J. *My Sense of Silence: Memoirs of a Childhood with Deafness*. Urbana, Ill.: Creative Nonfiction, 2000.

Flodin, Mickey. *Sign Language for Kids: The Fun Way for Anyone to Learn American Sign Language*. New York: Berkley, 1991.

Greene, Laura and Eva B. Dicker. *Sign-Me-Fine: Experiencing American Sign Language*. Washington, D.C.: Gallaudet University Press, 1991.

Landau, Elaine. *Deafness*. New York: Twenty-first Century, 1994.

Lowell, G. R. and K. S. Brooks. *Elana's Ears: Or, How I Became the Best Big Sister in the World*. New York: Dial, 1994.

Slier, D. *Word Signs*. Washington, D.C.: Gallaudet University Press, 1995.

Walker, Lou Ann. *Hand, Heart, and Mind: The Story of the Education of America's Deaf People*. New York: Dial, 1994.

Organizations and Online Sites

Deaf Library
http://www.deaflibrary.org/asl.html
This online site offers access to many articles on American Sign Language.

Lesson Tutor
http://www.lessontutor.com/ASLgenhome.html
Visitors to this site can receive lessons in basic communication with people who are deaf or hearing impaired.

Lifeprint Institute
http://www.lifeprint.com
This site offers an online course on American Sign Language.

Michigan State University
http://www.commtechlab.msu.edu/sites/aslweb/browser.html
Sponsored by the University of Michigan, this site is an online ASL dictionary, with video clips showing thousands of signs.

A Note on Sources

Many books have been invaluable in my research on American Sign Language. Especially informative about the history of ASL are *Forbidden Signs: American Culture and the Campaign against Sign Language* by Douglas C. Baynton and two excellent histories by Harlan Lane: *When the Mind Hears: A History of the Deaf* and *The Mask of Benevolence: Disabling the Deaf Community*. *The New Disability History: American Perspectives* edited by Paul K. Longmore and Lauri Umansky includes fascinating chapters on the sign or speech controversy. Nora Ellen Groce creates a rich portrait of the former deaf community on Martha's Vineyard in *Everyone Here Spoke Sign Language*. In *The Other Side of Silence: Sign Language and the Deaf Community in America*, Arden Neisser gives a thorough journalistic account of the ASL community. Paul Preston's *Mother Father Deaf: Living between Sound and Silence* is based on interviews with the hearing children of deaf parents.

A fine primer on ASL vocabulary and structure is *The Joy of Signing: American Sign Language and the Manual Alphabet* by Lottie Riekehof. More detailed explanations of ASL usage appear in *Linguistics of American Sign Language: An Introduction* by Clayton Valli and Ceil Lucas.

—*Deborah Kent*

Index

Numbers in *italics* indicate illustrations.

About the Author

Deborah Kent grew up in Little Falls, New Jersey, where she was the first blind student to attend the local public school. She received her B.A. in English from Oberlin College and a master's degree from Smith College School for Social Work.

To pursue her lifelong interest in writing, she moved to the town of San Miguel de Allende in Mexico, which had a thriving community of writers and artists.

While living in San Miguel, Ms. Kent helped to found the Centro de Crecimiento, the town's first school for children with disabilities. Many of the students were deaf, and Ms. Kent learned finger-spelling and some basic signs in order to communicate with them.

Ms. Kent is the author of more than a dozen young-adult novels, as well as numerous nonfiction titles for children. She lives in Chicago with her husband, children's author R. Conrad Stein, and their daughter Janna.